OLD PUBS OF NEWC

Geoff Phillips

Published by G P Electronic Services, 87 Willowtree Ave., Durham City, DH1 1DZ. Tel: 0191 384 9707
First published 1995

ISBN 0 9522480 4 2

Front cover design by Christine Phillips.
Text, Interior design, typesetting, and graphics by Geoff Phillips.
Printing of old photographs by Craig Oliphant.
Snippets of information about breweries by Len Winters.

Printed by:
Silverscreen Print plc.
Whinbank House, Whinbank Road, Aycliffe Industrial Estate, Newton Aycliffe, Co Durham, DL5 6AY.
Tel: 01325 300007

Front Cover photograph: Farmers Rest, Haymarket 1920. (Demolished 1995).

Acknowledgments:
The author would like to thank Jack Evans and George Mitchell for their help in recalling facts about many of the pubs featured in this book. Thanks also go to my father's friend and colleague Horsley Hall for contributing towards the book and checking the script.

Newcastle Arms, Clayton St 1915

The Newcastle Arms was a small pub located at the north end of Clayton Street where it met up with Blackett Street. This part of Clayton Street was demolished to make way for the Eldon Square Shopping Centre.

The pub was supplied by Swinburne and Company and served Bass and McEwans noted ales drawn from the wocd.

Grainger Hotel, Grainger St 1920

Richard Grainger was the man who, in the 1830's, was responsible for constructing many of the fine buildings which transformed Newcastle into a city of character and style. This photograph shows the hotel which took its name from the man himself. The hotel was located at the junction of Grainger Street and Market Street; in the 1970's the site was occupied by the Swears and Wells shop.

Prudhoe Arms, Corner Prudhoe St and Prudhoe Place 1920

This site is now occupied by Marks and Spencer's store and is where buses enter the bus station underneath the Eldon Square Shopping Centre. Other pubs on Prudhoe Street were Smiths Arms, Grapes Inn and County Inn.

Brass Man, Collingwood St 1972

Formerly known as the Shakespeare, the Brass Man was a Scottish and Newcastle house but originally a Robert Deuchar establishment. It was one of the few remaining pubs to have a men-only bar. It was demolished in 1974.

The Keg Beer "Shock Horror"

The 1970's saw the emergence of keg beer which was favoured by the youth of Newcastle but loathed by the more mature drinking man. Youngers Tartan was a hit with the students from Newcastle Polytechnic but was condemned by CAMRA members (The Campaign for Real Ale). They described keg beer as dead beer. All the sediment was removed and then the beer was pasteurised. Carbon dioxide was then forced in to give the beer its fizz. Many publicans liked it, however, as it kept longer and did not need as much care and attention as traditional cask conditioned beer.

Queens Head, Gallowgate 1930

Built in 1927, this fine building replaced the rather shabby pub of the same name.

Barras Bridge Hotel 1960's

Known locally as the "Sink" the Barras Bridge Hotel stood at the corner of Sandyford Road and Great North Road and it is rumoured that one of the pub's managers was known as Lord Vipond. Its postal address was No2 Great North Road. It was often frequented by visitors to the Town Moor fair. To the right, Newcastle's new Civic Centre is taking shape.

Jesmond Station Hotel, Sandyford Rd 1966

Further along Sandyford Road was the Lambert's Leap and then the Jesmond Station Hotel. They all met their demise when the new Civic Centre and surrounding roads were built.

Plough, Haymarket 1966

The Plough's address was actually 124 Percy Street. To the right is the building which housed the Haymarket Cinema and to the left is the Barbecue Express fast-food outlet which served chicken and chips long after most fish and chip shops closed on an evening in Newcastle's city centre. The Plough ceased trad ing in 1976.

What makes the perfect Tyneside pub?
This is what some Geordies had to say about the subject in the 1970's. Apart from the obvious - that is perfect beer, the barmaid should be friendly and greet you with a smile. Juke boxes should definitely go as they torture the eardrums and make conversation impossible. Juke boxes attract what beer drinkers call the "shandy set" - kids who shouldn't even be in a milk bar. Unwashed tables, full ashtrays and empty glasses everywhere count as high minus points and please don't clash my change down on the bar in a puddle of beer.

Crown & Sceptre
High Friar St 1966

Better known as Curley's Bar after the ex-boxer manager, the Crown and Sceptre was located in High Friar Street which was a narrow street which ran parallel to and to the south of Blackett Street. High Friar Street is no longer there as the area is now occupied by the Eldon Square Shopping Centre.

Other old pubs on High Friar Street:
Friars Cell
Lord Collingwood
Gardeners Arms.

Wellington, Collingwood St. 1900

The Wellington stood at the corner of Collingwood Street and Pudding Chare. In 1901 Barclays Bank bought the site and built a fine new building which still stands today.

Grapes Vaults, Grey St 1966

This pub was at the corner of Grey Street and High Friar Lane. The Trustee Savings Bank now occupies the site. To the right was Mawsons now Waterstones Bookshop.

Lord Stowell, Nelson St 1966

This pub took its name from the son of a Newcastle hoastman or coal-fitter called William Scott. His son, who was also called William, was educated at the Royal Grammar School and became Lord Stowell - Judge of the High Court of Admiralty.

Royal Albert, 49 Newgate St 1904

This view shows the corner of Newgate Street and Clayton Street looking south-west. Other old pubs on Newgate Street were Scotch Arms, Sun, Albion, Cumberland Arms, Victoria, Three Tuns, Phoenix, Chancellors Head, Lion & Lamb, Bacchus, Bull and Mouth and Bourgognes (was Masons Arms).

Locomotive, Westmorland Rd/Blenheim St 1966
This originally was a Higginbottom's pub.

Crown Hotel, Elswick Rd 1966

The Crown Hotel stood at the corner of Elswick Road and Bentinck Road.

Merry Monarch, Avison Street 1966

The Merry Monarch was at the corner of Avison Street and Douglas Terrace in an area of Newcastle known as Arthur's Hill which was named after Arthur Cookson who built most of the property in that area.

Stanhope House, Stanhope St 1920

Mitre, Stanhope St 1920
Standing at No. 165 Stanhope Street at the corner with Darnell Street was the Mitre. In the 1960's it was the Mitre Store.

Queen's Arms, Westgate Road 1966

Located at the corner of Elswick Row and Westgate Road, the Queen's Arms was yet another Scottish and Newcastle pub which met it's demise in the 1960's.

Bath Hotel, Corporation St 1966

This pub was right next door to Newcastle Breweries; needless to say the beer was spot on. The Breweries must have thought that the land was more useful to manufacture beer than to sell it and so a few years later down came the pub and up went some storage tanks.

Clock, Buckingham St 1966

A few yards further west was Buckingham Street and the Clock public house. Further downhill on this street was the Duke of Buckingham pub.

Hodgson Arms, Seaham St 1966

Located on the corner of Seaham Street and Oakes Lane, the Hodgson Arms was another Scottish and Newcastle house only a dart's throw from the brewery. The area is now taken up by a new yard for Newcastle Breweries' delivery vehicles.

William IV, Westgate Road 1966

At one point in time there were over two dozen pubs on Westgate Road. The William IV was approximately half way up the hill at the junction with Swinburne Place. The building now houses a second-hand store.

Marquis of Blandford, Westgate Road 1966

A few yards further downhill at the junction with Blandford Street was yet another S & N house. It was closed in 1971.

Waterloo, Westgate Road 1966

The Waterloo has just recently been demolished; it stood at the corner of Westgate Road and Bath Lane. To the right are sections of the City Wall.

North-Eastern, Westgate Rd 1930's

The North-Eastern was known as the Long Bar, probably because it stretched through to Neville Street behind. Right next door is the Douglas Hotel, which also met its demise in the early 70's.

Other ancient alehouses on Westgate Road were:

Duke of Gloucester
Cooksons Arms
Goat
Carliol House
Masons Arms
Pineapple
Talbot
Black Bull
Bay Horse
Crown
Times
Brandy Vaults
Criterion
Douglas Hotel
Express
Black Bulls Heads
Salutation
Midland
Gloucester
Talbot
Crown (second one)

Crown, Railway St 1966
A few yards east from the Globe (still standing) was the Crown at No. 1 Railway Street.

Lord Nelson, Trafalgar St 1966

Situated next door to the Trafalgar was the Lord Nelson, which looked as though it may have been a retail shop at one time.

Other pubs on Trafalgar Street going downhill from New Bridge Street, were:
Trafalgar
George Stephenson
New Railway Inn.

Royal Victoria, Melbourne St, 1966

Nicknamed the "Shamrock", this fine building stood at the corner of Melbourne Street and Blagdon Street. Another old pub on Melbourne Street was Red Barnes.

Duke of Argyle, Argyle St/Argyle Tce 1966

Nicknamed Paddy O'Malley's, this pub was located a few yards south of New Bridge Street. Further down Argyle Street was the Wallace Hotel.

Prince of Wales, Byron St Shieldfield 1966

The Prince of Wales stood at the corner of Byron Street and Northumberland Road.

Ridley Arms Hotel, Clarence St, Shieldfield 1966

Originally called Ridley Street before it became an extension to Clarence Street, it is situated near to New Bridge Street and St Dominic's Church. One of the managers there in the 1950's was Steve Lawlor. The lane to the right is Hewgill Terrace.

Melbourne, Ingham Place, Shieldfield 1966

Further along Hewgill Terrace at the junction with Ingham Place was the Melbourne, an S & N house serving McEwan's Scotch Ale. The pub was closed in 1973.

Mitre, Crawhall Road 1966

The Mitre was probably so named because of it's close proximity to St Dominic's Church further uphill to the right. The lane to the right was known as the Lumber'd and ran behind St Dominic's School. The area is now occupied by Red Barns Housing.

Globe Tavern, Buxton St 1920

This photograph shows the corner of Buxton Street and Melbourne Street close to an area known as the Battlefield. The Globe Tavern was taken over by the Co-operative Society and converted to a store. Another old pub on Buxton Street was Three Crowns.

Ropers Arms, Howard St 1966

Known locally as Quinney's, the Ropers Arms stood on Howard Street which connects Crawhall Road to Gibson Street and is situated behind the Tyne-Tees Television studios.

Rose and Crown, City Rd 1970

Probably frequented by staff of Tyne-Tees Television whose studios were directly across the road from this recently demolished Sir John Fitzgerald house. The last manager there was Jimmy Butterfield.

Other old pubs on City Road were Butchers Arms (Graham's) and the Albion nicknamed the "Brick Bar".

New Sun Inn, Quayside 1950

A Sir John Fitzgerald house which was known as Gilroy's in the 19th century but more recently nicknamed Holmes's after the manager. The author is seen to be starting young with the Geordie ritual of waiting for the pub to open on a Sunday morning.

Three Indian Kings, Quayside 1920

Located down a passageway from the Quayside, the Three Indian Kings was probably popular with seafaring men. The automobile is an old Morris Oxford with a "Dickie" at the back for carrying extra passengers.

Other Bygone Boozers on the Quayside:
Steamboat Inn
Scotch Arms
Bridge Inn
Turks Head
Ship
Royal Luncheon Bar
Queens Hotel.

Lord Nelson, Sandgate 1955
Sandgate was awash with pubs in the 19th century as it was the centre of the coal-shipping trade. The Lord Nelson, situated at the bottom of Johnson's entry, was one of the few remaining pubs on Sandgate in the 1950's and 60's.

Rose and Crown, Walker Road 1966

Further east, across Glasshouse Bridge we come to the start of Walker Road and the corner with St Lawrence Road. Here we see the Rose and Crown and the Free Trade Inn. The Free Trade is still in business but the Rose and Crown is now boarded up.

New Hawk Inn, Byker Bank 1966

A short journey north along Ford Street brings you to Byker Bank and the New Hawk Inn nicknamed Dyer Brown's, after the manager. The old Hawk was on the opposite side of the street. The New Hawk was built about 1881 and closed in 1967.

Burton House, Clifford St, Byker 1966

This pub was on the corner of Clifford Street and Burton Street just south from the top of Byker Bank. It was known locally as Tim Boag's, after the manager. Behind the photographer is St Silas Church. The pub was demolished in 1970.

Viaduct, Wilfred St, Byker 1966

Built around 1895, the Viaduct Hotel took its name from the new viaduct across the Ouseburn valley. The pub stood at the centre of Wilfred Street amongst a small close community which stretched down to Ouseburn Street in the valley. Like many other pubs in the area, it was often managed by ex-boxers, the last one being Ginger Roberts who came to the pub from the Queens Head in Shieldfield.

In its hey-day, Wilfred Street had three pubs, a theatre and a club. In between shows actors and staff from the Grand theatre would pop into the Viaduct for a pint of Deuchars ESP. In the 1960's many of the buildings on Wilfred Street were demolished but the pub survived for ten years after. The manager did not live in and consequently the pub suffered from attacks by vandals and thieves. In the 1970's the new Metro railway planners decided that a new bridge should pass directly through the site of the pub and so the bulldozers moved in.

Dues Bar, Dalton St, Byker 1960's

A few hundred yards further east at the corner of Dalton Street and Conyers Road was Dues Bar, formerly the Royal Station Hotel and nicknamed Billy Burns.

Ellison Arms Hotel, Felling View, St Anthonys 1920's

Located at the bottom of Pottery Bank, the Ellison Arms stood on Felling View, formerly Ropery Walk. It was situated at a bend in the River Tyne overlooking Felling. New housing has now been built on the site.

Lord Raglan Inn, Felling View, St Anthonys 1966
Just a few yards down the road from the Ellison Arms Hotel was the Lord Raglan Inn, named after the famous English General who lost an arm in the Battle of Waterloo.

Davy Inn, Davy Bank, Wallsend 1966

Said to have been Wallsend's oldest pub, the Davy Inn was run by the Coxon family. In the bar was a miniature pair of boxing gloves which were said to have been made from Jack Dempsey's boxing gloves which he wore on his last fight in 1927.

Crown and Anchor, Fisher St, Walker 1966

Located opposite the entrance to Swan Hunter's "middle yard", this pub was bought by Joe Besterfield of Algernon Road in the 1920's and managed by George Anderson.

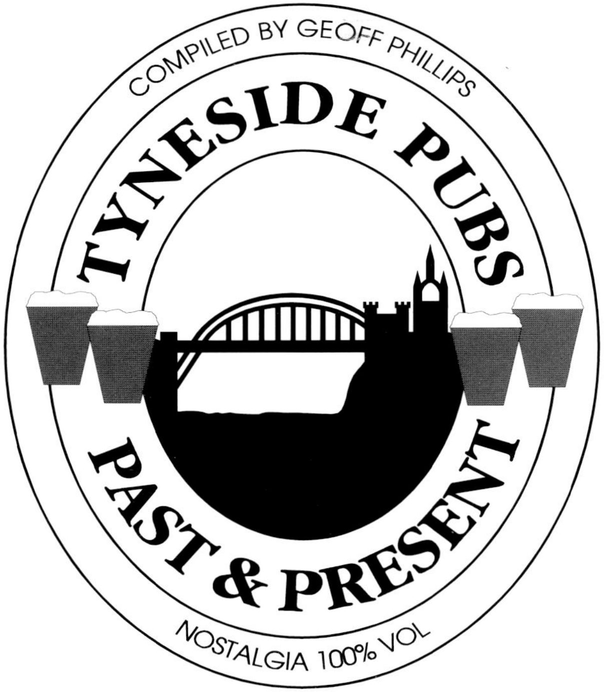

Further reading

Tyneside Pubs: Past and Present

A Bridge Inn Time

by
Geoff Phillips

Tyneside Pubs: Past and Present is another book in the hugely successful Past and Present series. It presents the reader with a nostalgic pictorial pub-crawl through time and Tyneside. More photographs from the Jack Phillips Collection show pubs in Newcastle and its suburbs as they were in days gone by, along with modern photographs showing how things have changed. A pub quiz is included to test the reader's knowledge of bygone boozers.

Over 100 photographs of Tyneside as it used to be, alongside similar views of the present day.
Intriguing facts and information about each photograph and maps showing the locations of selected pubs.
ISBN 0 9522480 2 6. Retail Price: £6.95. Obtainable where you bought this book.

Publisher and Distributor: G P Electronic Services, 87 Willowtree Ave. Durham DH1 1DZ